PRAYING
WITH CONFIDENCE

Renewing Your Trust and Joy in God

DAVID EGNER

PRAYING
WITH CONFIDENCE

Renewing Your Trust and Joy in God

DISCOVERY HOUSE
P U B L I S H E R S °

Feeding the Soul with the Word of God

P.O. Box 3566, Grand Rapids MI 49501-3566

Requests for permission to quote from this book
should be directed to:
Permission Department
Discovery House Publishers
P.O. Box 3566
Grand Rapids, MI 49501

Scripture quotations are from the
New King James Version.
Copyright © 1982 by Thomas Nelson, Inc.
Used by permission. All rights reserved.

Cover design by Stan Myers
Cover photo by Getty Images
Interior design by Steve Gier

ISBN: 978-1-57293-504-4

Printed in the United States of America

11 12 13 14 15 / DPI_RBC / 7 6 5 4 3 2 1

CONTENTS

INTRODUCTION

P RAYER IS TOUGH. For followers of Christ, we know we are supposed to pray, and the Bible challenges us to pray—but sometimes we wonder if it really matters. If it's really worth it. After all, we have all prayed prayers that were not answered the way we wanted or at the time we wanted them to be answered. We have all encountered friends and loved ones who felt that their prayers had risen no higher than the proverbial ceiling.

In times like these, disappointment can take over our hearts and lead us to decide that prayer is pointless.

But is that the end of the story? Do moments of disappointment or question replace the assurances that we find in the pages of God's book, or is it actually possible to find good reason for confidence in our prayers? Is praying just a crutch for people too weak to fully and courageously engage life, or could it be the dynamic link with our heavenly Father that we desperately crave? Those are valid questions worthy of careful thought and consideration.

The purpose of this book is to help reawaken confidence in the wisdom of God, trust in the character of God, and hope in the plan of God. It is to remind us why prayer is more than just a religious exercise—it is a personal opportunity to experience the greatness of God. We encourage you to consider the possibility that prayer is more about exclamation points than question marks. It really is possible to pray with confidence in God and His love.

—BILL CROWDER
Associate Bible Teacher, RBC Ministries

The
TROUBLE
WITH PRAYER

I N FRONT OF ME SAT A GROUP of adult singles
who were gathered to do a study on prayer.
I handed out a sheet of paper that began
with this statement:

"When it comes to prayer, I _____
_____." They were to fill in the blank.

How would you fill in the rest of that sentence?

Before we go on, it might be helpful for you
to answer that question. Think carefully about
your prayer life and complete this sentence:

When it comes to prayer, I _____

_____.

When I tabulated what the group had written, the results fell into these categories:

- "I don't pray enough."
- "I don't know what to pray."
- "I don't know if prayer does any good."

I've found such answers common. While a few Christians I talk to about prayer will speak glowingly of the ease with which they slip in and out of conversations with God, most seem to view prayer as a struggle that is sometimes won but more often lost.

It is understandable that prayer would not always come easily. Rightly understood, it is not just emotion addressed to God. It is so much more.

- Prayer is an expression of faith that is often weak and small.
- Prayer is a weapon of spiritual warfare that is used to fight for contested ground.

• Prayer is a reflection of a relationship with God that is often disrupted and strained by our own ignorance, inattention, and insensitivity.

• Prayer is an expression of confidence in God that is often replaced by feelings of disappointment.

Often our prayer experience changes as we move through the stages of our Christian life. For instance, perhaps early in our Christian walk we pray with high expectations. We assume that God will give us the deepest desires of our heart and that through prayer we will experience the closeness and happiness we long for. With our fresh, new confidence in God we believe that we will rise above any problem.

Then as time goes by something happens. Maybe we ask God for something important to us and we don't get it. We assure ailing friends that we are praying for their recovery, but they don't get better. We pray in the presence of our family for a solution to problems that are affecting them, only to be left waiting for months and months while God seems to ignore us. We plead earnestly and often for our loved ones' spiritual restoration, but they remain cold toward God.

Slowly, disappointment forms. We lose our enthusiasm for prayer. Soon we're praying only at mealtimes. We go through a phase when we won't bring anything we care about to the Lord because we can't take another rejection. Instead of bringing everything to God in prayer, we go to the other extreme. We stop communicating with Him at all.

Think a minute about your prayer relationship with God. Are you somewhere on that track? Maybe you haven't stopped completely, but you can feel your fervor for prayer waning. If that has happened—if you've stopped growing in prayer, is it because of honest disappointment?

• *Disappointment with God.* "I asked and believed that God was going to heal my daughter. But she lost her fight with cancer anyway. I'm brokenhearted and confused." You trusted God with your toughest circumstances. You took your requests to Him in faith, yet things have not gone well. The pain you are suffering because of the loss in your life is compounded by your confusion about what good it does to talk to God. You read about answers to prayer in Scripture, and you've heard stories about it among the people you know. But for you, your urgent pleadings have not borne the fruit you were asking to receive.

• *Disappointment with others.* "I have a hard time praying when I am so angry with people who are ruining my life." You know you cannot control others—perhaps children who are living apart from God and ruining their lives or maybe friends with whom you've had a falling out that you didn't want—but you assumed that God could intervene and help those people. But they keep moving away from you, and your prayers can't seem to make them stop and turn around.

• *Disappointment with ourselves.* "I've wanted to pray. I've looked forward to it. I've had the best of intentions. But I just haven't been able to get around to it." Life is busy. Life is complicated. Life is sometimes full of distractions. And amidst it all, it seems impossible to get away to spend time with God. Every time you try to get seriously involved in prayer, the phone rings or your mind wanders or you fall asleep. You end up kicking yourself again because prayer just isn't working like it should.

If these kinds of things are troubling you, think of it like this: It takes faith and courage to work thorough a disrupted human relationship. Think about times when you were disappointed with a friend, a spouse, a child. It was not easy to repair that relationship so you could again communicate in a calm, productive way. If someone has not delivered on a promise or has seemingly let you down, it takes a process to reestablish what you once had. And perhaps you've caused a rift between you and a loved one—and you know it's your fault. Even when you took steps to restore the connection, it took effort to patch things up.

In many regards, it's the same in our relationship with God. The first step in restoring fellowship with Him in prayer is to admit the problem. Then we must work past the disappointment and regain our confidence in God and even in prayer itself.

In effect, we need to return in our lives to the place the disciples were when they sat down with the Master and said to Him, "Lord, teach us to pray." We need to then sit at his feet and listen to His instructions provided throughout the Bible.

This book has been written to help you if you have lost confidence in prayer. It is our prayer that as you listen to God's instructions through what talking to Him can

.... our lives that you will regain the confidence you once had in the marvelous avenue of communication with God called prayer.

A Personal Story: Praying for Nathan

But before we go on, let me speak personally for a moment. I know a little of what it means to be disappointed with the twists and turns of life. Sometimes the most disturbing experiences have involved what God has allowed in the lives of those closest to my heart.

One of those times involved the health of a dear grandson. Nathan was born with an immune deficiency. His tiny body had no mechanism for fighting disease. In the first few years of his life, we watched helplessly as little Nathan struggled through a series of upper respiratory infections.

Of course, we petitioned God for help. Our family and our church family all joined together in prayer. However, God didn't seem to be answering our pleas. Hospitalizations were common.

As a family we were frightened. Could we trust God even if He didn't answer our prayers for this one so dear to our hearts?

Doctors told us that the immune system in 60 percent of these children "kicks in" about the time they turn 3. While that information offered some hope, it also left us with the realization that 40 percent of them do not develop defenses against infection. Time after time, I looked at that defenseless little boy and prayed.

At first I was consumed by the "what ifs" of Nathan's condition. As time went on, the focus of my prayers changed. I was no longer as absorbed in the pain I was feeling. I found myself using fewer words. I wrestled, often in silence, on Nathan's behalf. Eventually I was saying simply, "God, do what's best. Only You know, and I trust You and Your goodness. I want so much for You to heal him. Yet, Your will be done."

About the time Nate turned 3, he began to have fewer infections. Then new tests came back: God mercifully let Nathan be one of the 60 percent who overcome immune deficiency.

Through such uncontrollable circumstances of life I have been learning to trust God in the school of prayer. Sometimes I have been grateful for His "yes." Sometimes I've even learned to enjoy God in the process of waiting for His answer.

Yet I still find myself lapsing into the discouragement of circumstances. I find myself longing for the kind of power that would give me Elijah-like control over physical conditions. James tells us that Elijah, that Old Testament man of faith and miracles, was no different from us. He was "a man with a nature like ours" (5:17), yet his prayers caused God to turn off the rain. He was an example of what James called "a righteous man" whose "effectual, fervent prayer" did a lot of good (5:16). Who doesn't want to be like Elijah?

What I've learned in time, however, is that real confidence in prayer isn't found by projecting my desires upon God. Instead, I have found confidence by learning some simple yet profound principles of prayer. They do not depend on our ability to be eloquent or spiritually insightful. They have ABC-like qualities that are learned in our Lord's school of prayer.

21

RETURNING
to the
BASICS

IMAGINE FOR A MOMENT that you were able to achieve the early confidence in prayer that often accompanies new faith in Christ—the refreshing, powerful feeling that for the first time in your life you had the ear of the master of the universe. Think about what it would mean to know that you could have a conversation with a heavenly Father who loved you so much that He gave up His Son for you and who has promised to care for you for an eternity.

Contemplate how that could transform your life, renew your trust in God, and rekindle the joy of your relationship with Him.

Sometimes when we want to accomplish something profound in our lives, we start with the basic steps. For example, going on a diet seems daunting, but if the process is broken into its basics and those basics are followed, little by little the pounds go away or the good health returns. Same with prayer. If you need to return to more confidence in your prayer life, start with the basics, and see how through small steps you can return to the trust and joy you know is possible.

A | Approach God Through a Mediator

Mediation was God's idea. He knew we had a problem trusting Him. But He could not ignore what we were doing. So God offered mediation. To resolve the differences that had come between us, He sent One who could understand and be sympathetic to our condition while at the same time representing the interests of heaven.

This Mediator so identified with us and became so involved in our problems that He made the ultimate sacrifice for us. He suffered so greatly on our behalf on a cross of execution that as He hung suspended between heaven and earth He ended up crying out, "My God, My God, why have your forsaken Me?" (Mark 15:34). In the darkest hour of human history, this Mediator experienced not only the pain and suffering of our sins on His shoulders but also the feeling of being utterly alone in the universe.

Yet, just three days after that inexpressible moment, it became clear that the Mediator had been victorious. Through His great sacrifice, our Mediator had removed the barrier that had disrupted our relationship with God. By this selfless action, a line of communication was now open by which we could fellowship with

God—indeed, we could become a member of God's family. The Mediator who opened the door to a relationship with God was Jesus, whose death, burial, and resurrection gave us the chance to commune with the holy God of the universe.

We would still sin. We would still be blinded by our own desires and stubborn pride. We would still find ourselves filled with regret. We would still become confused about what God was doing in our lives. But never again would we have reason to doubt the Father's love for us. Never again could it be persuasively argued that the Father didn't care, that He wasn't touched by our problems, or that He had left us to die in our hopeless circumstances.

And most important for the purposes of this study, never again would we have to approach God in prayer without the assurance that He wanted to talk with us far more than we wanted to talk to Him.

Without this mediatorial work of the Savior, we might have wondered if God would even listen to us when we prayed. We might assume from our circumstances that He didn't care. But now the memory of what happened on the Mediator's cross can restore our confidence whenever we approach God in prayer. Now we can take courage in the fact that we don't have to approach God in our own sin-stained reputation. We don't come to Him in our own name. We don't approach Him with our own carefully chosen words. We come to Him in the merits of the One who paid the price of our sins with His own blood. We come to God in the name and interests of His own dearly loved Son, Jesus Christ.

Consider the confidence this gives us as we prepare to enter into prayer. We can look back over the years and reflect on Jesus' work for us as an indication of His love, and we can also look at our circumstances of today and realize that Jesus' death guarantees the fact that we will always have an advocate with the Father.

The Confidence In A Past Sacrifice

This manner of approach has always been in God's mind for us. Long before our Mediator's arrival, the design for such an approach to God was illustrated in the tabernacle and temple worship of Israel. For many centuries God had made it clear that His people must approach Him on the basis of a blood sacrifice. But only in the coming and suffering of Christ do we see that those sacrifices pointed toward the violent suffering and death of God's own Son.

In both the tabernacle used by the Israelites on their wilderness journey toward the Promised Land and in the temple later built in Jerusalem, God instructed the people to construct a place that signified the very Presence of God. And in that place was an altar of incense. The burning incense on that altar, by its fragrance and ascending motion, symbolized prayers that please God.

28

Significantly, this incense was lit by a coal from another implement in the tabernacle—the altar of sacrifice (Exodus 30:7-10). In God's mind, there is a connection between the sacrifice and the prayers by which we approach Him.

This link between sacrifice and prayer is what our Mediator secured for us. On the cross, He offered a sacrifice that was acceptable to God. By virtue of that sacrifice, He encouraged us to go into the presence of God in His own name. Of this basis for confidence, the author of Hebrews wrote:

29

> Seeing then that we have a great High Priest who has passed through the heavens, Jesus the Son of God, let us hold fast our confession. For we do not have a High Priest who cannot sympathize with our weaknesses, but was in all points tempted as we are, yet without sin. Let us therefore come boldly to the throne of grace, that we may obtain mercy and find grace to help in time of need (Hebrews 4:14-16).

Being in the presence of God is described in this passage as like being in a throne room.

In Europe and the Middle East, the throne rooms of kings were ornately and elaborately decorated and filled with attendants. Fixtures were covered with gold. Purple material draped the throne and was hung throughout the room. The throne itself was elevated above the level upon which commoners walked. The seat of power was central to the room, and everything pointed toward it and the king who sat upon it.

Any common people who might find occasion to enter the throne room would have felt inferior and intimidated. These are the very feelings we might have as we approach God in prayer—if we did not have a Mediator to give us confidence. But through the mediation, the sacrifice, the resurrection, and the understanding of Christ, all who have placed their faith in Him can walk confidently into the presence of God without feeling like an unwanted intruder in some ostentatious, off-limits throne room.

We come in the name and merits of the Son of God, and that gives us access to the Father at any time. We have an invitation, stamped with the royal seal, to pray at any time, under any conditions, whatever our circumstances or needs, because this new throne room is a welcoming "throne of grace." Grace, which is undeserved kindness. Grace, which is unmerited assistance. Grace by which we have become members of God's family—giving us the right to enter that throne room without intimidation. This is the kind of help our Mediator has secured for us.

The Confidence In A Present Advocate

There's even more! We can come to "the throne of grace" with confidence in our Mediator because His work for us continues. While Jesus' actual sacrifice for us took place in real time 2,000 years ago, its effect has crossed the centuries to today. Even now He is at the right hand of God pleading on our behalf. Paul explained it like this:

"It is Christ who died, and furthermore is also risen, who is even at the right hand of God, who also makes intercession for us" (Romans 8:34).

On the merit of His sacrifice, the Lord Jesus became then and remains now our Intercessor and Advocate.

He is with the Father in the throne room of heaven, speaking on our behalf. The apostle John expressed it this way:

If anyone sins, we have an Advocate with the Father, Jesus Christ the righteous. And He Himself is the propitiation [the atoning sacrifice] for our sins (1 John 2:1-2).

Why do we hold back? How could we feel hesitant or unworthy to pray when Jesus Christ himself, on the basis of His sacrifice for us, is right now with the Father pleading our case?

Once we grasp the idea of going to God in prayer and once we develop the confidence we need to approach Him because of Jesus' sacrifice and His advocacy, we need to consider how we talk with the heavenly Father—still keeping in mind the confidence we can have in Him.

B | Be Honest About Your Complaints

God loves honest talk. Realism is at the heart of His own character. He hates darkness and deception. Darkness is the domain of His enemy. Therefore, a second essential to confidence in prayer is to learn to be honest and open about what is in our hearts. He can handle our complaints, our foolishness, our fears, and our failures. He won't be surprised or threatened by our anger, our confusion, or our childlike pleadings.

One person has asked rhetorically, "Has it ever occurred to you that nothing has ever occurred to God?" In other words, our omnipotent heavenly Father is already aware of what is on our hearts, so there is no reason to hold back as we ask for

33

His help. And He is much better equipped to handle our problems than we are. Therefore, it pleases God for us to open our hearts to Him.

What does not please God are the cheap lies of flattery, ritual praise, and insincere words repeated over and over (Matthew 6:7) without regard for what is really happening in our own soul. We need to put away our practices of fearful coverup, our sophisticated deceit, and our formal language. Instead, we need to lay the foundation of truth as the basis for prayer.

Prayers filled with pious lies are unacceptable to God, and they do not reflect the true spirit of our own hearts.

In order to enter the throne room of grace and begin to pray with confidence, we must learn to be truthful when we pray. To do this, we have to spend time in self-evaluation and confession of sin. We must tell God how we really feel about Him, about ourselves, about our problems with people, and about our needs, frustrations, desires, and painful memories. We must also be honest about our desire to know His will and make it our own. If we don't want to do His will, then that too must be brought to light so we can ask God to help us overcome our rebellion and foolishness.

Our efforts to speak truthfully and honestly with God can serve as guiding lights toward building our confidence in prayer.

Confidence In God's Ability To Help Us Understand Ourselves

When we want to know the truth about ourselves, the Lord who knows our hearts will help us to see what is happening in us. The psalmist wrote, "O Lord, You have searched me and known me" (Psalm 139:1). David said to Solomon, "The Lord searches all hearts and understands all the intent of the thoughts" (1 Chronicles 28:9).

The prayer of self-examination, when combined with the Scriptures, enables us to see what's really going on inside. The Bible shows us our deep-seated feelings and true motives. It takes us into the nooks and crannies where we hide old grudges and secret hatreds and bitter resentments. It shows us places of the heart that are dark, and it shows us attitudes of the mind that need to be refreshed and pointed God-ward.

Through honest prayer we can bring these things to the surface, see them for what they really are, and ask God to help us deal with them.

Of this we can be confident: If we ask God to show us our hearts, He will do it. David's plea for transparency in Psalm 139:23 should guide our own similar plea: "Search me, O God," he said, "and know my heart; try me, and know my anxieties." Perhaps this will not happen immediately. But over time and in His own way, the Lord will pull back the curtains of denial and repression and show us ourselves. And He will take good care of us while He's doing it.

• He might bring an old hurt to mind for us

to deal with and forget.

• He might remind us of a promise we have not kept or a debt we have not paid.

• He might let us feel the hurt we gave to someone else, perhaps many years ago, and tell us to make it right.

• He might direct us to straighten out a misunderstanding or forgive someone.

Heart knowledge is a wonderful, liberating gift, and it comes through being honest with the Lord in prayer.

Self-examination can also reveal the positive blessings in our lives. God is working in us and doing things for us all the time. He shows us His goodness, fills us with grace, helps us grow through adversity, sustains us through difficult circum-stances, gives us ways to escape temptation, and grants us His peace. But when we're caught up in the details of life and distracted by responsibilities, we are sometimes oblivious to these things.

Confidence In God's Willingness To Forgive An Honest Heart

It was the bottom of the ninth inning and the score was tied. The opposing team had the bases loaded with two outs. A hard ground ball was hit a little to the right of the rookie shortstop. He got into position, reached down to field the ball, but it bounced off his glove and into left field. The run scored and the game was lost. The shortstop had made that play a thousand times before—but not that time.

That ballplayer could have done what a lot of us do. He could have claimed that the ball hit a rock and took a bad bounce. He could have blamed the sun or the wet grass. But he didn't. "I blew it," he said after the game. "I take responsibility. It was my fault."

We need that attitude toward God. When the Lord convicts us of sin, we need to admit it, confess it, and then believe in God's willingness to forgive us.

Do you remember the biblical story of David and Nathan? It can teach us the value of recognizing sin and then confessing it as a way of getting back into right fellowship with God.

Corrupted by the power of the monarchy, David turned his duties, namely, fighting a war with the Ammonites, over to his commander-in-chief Joab and stayed at home in Jerusalem while the men went out to battle.

While other kings were off fighting wars (2 Samuel 11:1-2), David was lounging at home. One night, he got up from his bed and began wandering around the rooftop of the palace. From his vantage point, he noticed a woman taking a bath. The temptation was too much for him, and he began looking lustfully at this bathing beauty; Scripture says she was "very beautiful to behold" (v. 2).

The king summoned one of his men, probably a bodyguard, to find out who this woman was. The man replied with a question, "Is this not Bathsheba, the daughter of Eliam, the wife of Uriah the Hittite?" Next, David took his lust to another level. He sent messengers to have her brought to the palace, where he had sexual relations with this wife of one of his fighting men.

This adulterous relationship led to Bathsheba's pregnancy, and David was trapped in a lair of his own making. He attempted to cover up his sin by bringing Uriah home from battle so he could be with his wife—in an attempt to make it appear that her pregnancy was Uriah's doing. The noble fighting man, however, refused to sleep in his own house while his fellow soldiers were in battle— which ruined David's coverup.

Therefore, the king came up with an alternate plan—one that was amazing in its cold-heartedness. He called on his commander-in-chief Joab to make sure Uriah was on the frontlines of the battle. David even called for Uriah to have other soldiers back off to leave

40

him so vulnerable that he would be killed.

The plan worked, and a good man's life was taken because of David's sin and schemes.

Bathsheba mourned the death of her husband for some time. But after the mourning period was over, David called for her to be brought into the palace. There he married her.

While it may have appeared that David was about to get away with murder, the Lord sent a man named Nathan to visit the king. The visitor told David a story—a parable—about a rich man who took a poor man's prized lamb and served it up to a traveler who had come to visit. When David heard this story, he was appalled by the audacity of the rich man. His "anger was greatly aroused" (2 Samuel 12:5). But then Nathan stunned the king with these undeniable words of condemnation, "You are the man!" (v. 7).

Finally, after days and probably many months of living in self-imposed darkness, David acknowledged his sin. He said to Nathan, who had

41

delivered God's pointed condemnation of David's sin, "I have sinned against the Lord" (v. 13).

Later, David recorded His moving prayer of repentance in Psalm 51. "I acknowledge my transgressions," he confessed to the Lord, "and my sin is always before me. Against You, You only, have I sinned" (vv. 3-4). David pleaded for a restoration to the joy he once had. "Create in me a clean heart," he prayed, "and renew a steadfast spirit within me. Do not cast me away from Your presence, and do not take Your Holy Spirit from me. Restore to me the joy of my salvation" (vv. 10-12). His prayer was answered by the forgiveness of God.

The Bible, the Holy Spirit, and God's people serve as our Nathans today.

We live in a calloused world of hardened hearts and desensitized consciences. Lawyers can argue cases with skill and apparent sincerity even when they know the defendant is guilty. Sentences for horrible crimes are received without a sign of guilt or remorse. We are experts at denial and rationalization and finding someone else to blame.

How can we soften our hearts when all around us is such hardness? We're so accustomed to an iron-shelled coldness. How do we get "a broken and a contrite heart" (Psalm 51:17) that is always accepted by the Lord? We ask for it. "Create in me a clean heart," we must plead—just as David did. When we have sinned, each of us must petition God to "renew a steadfast spirit within me" (v.10). God will honor that prayer.

43

He didn't turn away when David asked for forgiveness, and He won't turn away when we pray, "God, be merciful to me a sinner!" (Luke 18:13).

Confidence In God's Ability To Handle Our Complaints

Our human relationships are cluttered with disagreements, struggles, and conflict. If there are none, it just might be that someone is suppressing a difficulty and postponing a confrontation until the future. Friends and spouses who have successful relationships learn to talk about their negative feelings openly and work through their differences—not hide them and keep them bottled up. This should also be true in our relationship with God. We are free to respectfully and reverently disagree, question, and even argue with Him in prayer.

Rabbi Joseph Telushkin writes of the need for honest confrontations with God as being a legacy of the Jewish people. In his book *Jewish Literacy* he writes:

> [The] first instance of a human being arguing with God becomes a characteristic feature of the Hebrew Bible, and of Judaism in general. Hundreds of years after Abraham, the psalmist called out to God in anger and anguish: "Awake! Why do You sleep, O Lord? . . . Why do You hide Your face, and forget our affliction and our oppression?" (Psalm 44:23-24; see Habakkuk 1:2 and the entire

book of Job for other examples of prophets
or righteous men questioning God's ways).
The willingness to confront the Almighty
stems from the belief that God, like man, has
responsibilities, and deserves criticism when
He fails to fulfill them. Elie Wiesel, a Jew who
stands in this tradition, has declared: "The
Jew may love God, or he may fight with God,
but he may not ignore God."

This seems to have been Abraham's attitude.
God was about to destroy the wicked city of
Sodom. Abraham interceded with the Lord, asking that the city be spared if fifty righteous people
could be found. He said, "Would you also destroy
the righteous with the wicked? Suppose there
were fifty righteous within the city; would You
also destroy the place and not spare it for the fifty
righteous that were in it?" (Genesis 18:23-24).

"So the Lord said, 'If I find in Sodom fifty
righteous within the city, then I will spare all the
place for their sake' " (v. 26).

45

Abraham was not done. Step by step, Abraham pleaded with God to reduce the number to ten righteous people in Sodom. But when ten could not be found, Sodom was destroyed (vv. 23-33).

Moses also disagreed with God. The Lord had performed miracle after miracle to deliver Israel from Egyptian bondage and provide for the Israelites in the wilderness. But while Moses was in the heights of Mount Sinai receiving from the Lord the Ten Commandments, the regulations for Jewish life, and the specifications for the tabernacle, his countrymen were getting ready to give up on the One who had delivered them from Egypt.

In violation of the first commandment God had given to them through Moses, they made an idol of gold and used it as an excuse to indulge in the sexual abandon of pagan fertility worship.

While Moses was still on the mountain, God said to him, "Go, get down! For your people . . . have corrupted themselves" (Exodus 32:7).

After calling the Israelites "a stiff-necked people" (v. 9), God seemed ready to wipe them off the face of the desert.

"Now therefore, let Me alone," God said to Moses, "that My wrath may burn hot against them and I may consume them" (Exodus 32:10). God even said He would start over again and make a great nation out of Moses.

However, Moses didn't want to give in. He pleaded with the Lord on behalf of the people. He said, "Why should the Egyptians speak, and say, 'He brought them out to harm them, to kill them in the mountains, and to consume them from the face of the earth'? Turn from Your fierce wrath, and relent from this harm to Your people" (v. 12). God relented, and the Jews were spared (v. 14).

Abraham and Moses are good examples for us. We too can clear the air with God. While still fearing God and remembering to reverence Him, we can also do the following:

- Ask Him why He's waiting so long to save

our loved one.

- Express our anger and disappointment because our child was not spared.
- Pour out our frustration to Him because we haven't found a job yet.
- Cry out to Him because we are still childless.

Such complaints and others like them do not threaten God. He knows we will never find a moral weakness in Him. He encourages us to be honest with Him so we can discover the thoughts and feelings that are in our hearts. Once we bring them to the light, we can ask God to help us deal with them.

So, why are we so hesitant to be honest with God? With such clear evidence from Scripture that God wants our genuine expressions of respectful expression in prayer, why do we hold back? Perhaps we're the kind of people who avoid all conflict. We won't even tell our loved ones or friends any of our negative feelings. Or we may think it would be a lack of faith to challenge God.

Many of us have accepted society's idea that struggle and love do not go together. We assume that a relationship is good only as long as there is nothing but peace and harmony. The fact remains that one of the reasons we struggle in relationships is because we really do care. And finding the courage to struggle and take risks and confront in the right way is one thing that strengthens and deepens all relationships. The same is true in our relationship with God. Like Jacob at Bethel, we would do well to wrestle with God once in a while. It can bring us His blessing (Genesis 32:24-32).

49

Confidence In What God Wants For Us

The goal of the believer in Jesus Christ is to become one (in heart and agreement) with God. When we come to Him in prayer, we need to be honest with ourselves about whether our desires are His desires, whether our will is His will, and whether our requests would be His requests.

How do we grow in this "oneness" with God?

Certainly we can never share in His complete understanding of all things. Yet as we pray for the daily needs of life, for our spouse and children and friends, for healing or employment or guidance, we can do so with the same attitude of heart Jesus had in mind when He taught His disciples to pray.

In answer to the question of one of His disciples, Jesus first told His listeners how to address God as their Father in heaven. Then he reminded them to show reverence for His name by saying, "Hallowed be Your name" (Matthew 6:9) and to look forward to God's great kingdom that is to come (v. 10). And then Jesus reminded His disciples of the importance of putting their confidence in God's plans with this part of the prayer: "Your will be done on earth as it is in heaven" (v. 10).

Jesus Himself expressed that same attitude a few hours before His death. He concluded an agonizing prayer session in the Garden of Gethsemane—a time when He even asked the

Father to let Him avoid the cross—with these words: "Nevertheless not My will, but Yours, be done" (Luke 22:42). This surrender, after an intense, honest struggle, kept Him in a spirit of oneness with His Father.

We may have questions about praying, "Your will be done." Does that mean we are secretly giving up on what we just prayed for? Are we not saying that our prayer was offered without the true conviction that it was right and that God should answer it? Are we not falsely humble in trying not to bother God with our little wishes, and saying, "That's okay. I understand," if He does not grant our requests? If so, we've got it all wrong!

Helmut Thielicke wrote:

This [the previous sentence] is just what the words "Thy will be done" do not mean. They mean, "Thou understandest my prayer better than I understand it myself (Romans 8:26). Thou knowest most whether I need hunger or bread. Whatever may come, I will still say,

'Yes, dear Lord' (Matthew 15:27). For I know that in everything, no matter what it may be, Thy will gives me fulfillment—beyond my asking and my comprehension."

When we pray "Your will be done," we are choosing to agree with God. We are saying to Him what Jesus said to His disciples, "My food is to do the will of Him who sent Me" (John 4:34). And we are echoing the Lord's prayer in Gethsemane. Whether or not He gives us bread or a job or a mate or a child, His will—done His way—is best.

We will not discover the confidence of being in agreement with God, however, if we have not first been honest about the thoughts and emotions of our own hearts. Integrity of soul is basic to overcoming disappointment with God and developing confidence in prayer.

C | Converse Instead Of Talk

A common hindrance to confident praying is the

feeling that no one is listening. We feel like the wife who tries to talk to her husband while he is reading the sports page of the newspaper or the father who is talking to his teenagers while they are plugged in to their iPods. No feedback, no response, not even an occasional, "Uh-huh."

When we feel that this kind of thing is happening in our prayer life, we begin to see prayer as nothing more than an empty ritual. We start to think that our words simply bounce off the ceiling and do us no good whatsoever.

53

We run the danger of losing sight of a vital truth: God is deeply interested in us, and He is listening intently to every word of our prayers. We might forget that prayer is intended to be a spirited interaction between us and a loving Being with whom we have an intimate and growing relationship. "We have almost forgotten," wrote A. W. Tozer in *Pursuit Of God,* "that God is a person and, as such, can be cultivated [in a relationship] as any person can."

When we feel that God is not listening, we need to focus on two vital aspects of prayer.

Confidence In Listening To God

Prayer is not merely what we say to God. It is also responding thoughtfully to what He has already said and what He is constantly saying to us through His Word. For this reason, the Bible is an important part of our ongoing conversation with the Lord.

54

One way to develop conversation with God is to open the Scriptures to a psalm or a paragraph from one of the Epistles. Read a passage thoughtfully to discover what the text is telling you about the thoughts, affections, and values of God. Listen carefully and reverently to the mind of the One who inspired these words. Ask Him to help you discover the interests and desires of His heart. Then respond conversationally from your own heart to what you are hearing. As you do, you will begin to develop confidence that you know what is important to God.

You will also begin to discover what God is doing in your own heart.

For an example of how this can work, look at 1 Corinthians 13. Suppose a husband has been reading this "love chapter," and he wants to pray in response to the words he has experienced. In prayer, he asks God to help him be the husband God wants him to be. Then he reads and listens:

"Love suffers long" (v.4). God speaks in those words to the man, reminding him of the times he has been impatient with his wife—even to the point of getting angry with her if she takes too long to make a decision, answer a question, or even get ready for church. In those words, God is speaking truth to the husband and telling him that He values patience in a relationship.

Continuing on into the passage, any of us can hear God speaking to us, and when we pray these words or others in Scripture, we can dialog with God about what He wants us to know and

55

how He wants us to live.

Changes in attitude and behavior can come to us if we listen to what God has already said to us in a passage such as this. If we read and listen, God speaks.

"Be silent," one seventeenth-century theologian wrote, "and listen to God. Let your heart be in such a state of preparation that His Spirit may impress upon you such virtues as will please Him. This silence of all outward and earthly affection and of human thoughts within us is essential if we are to hear this voice."

It won't be an audible voice. But you will know it's the voice of the Spirit when you hear the truths of Scripture speaking gently, lovingly, and forcefully to the circumstances and concerns of your life.

One night when my grandson Nathan was extremely ill, I awakened and prayed for him. While I remained in an attitude of prayer, silent before the Lord, I became aware of something else: a way I had not been sensitive to the needs of my wife, Shirley. I began to see how my attitudes had not been in line with the words and heart of God. I recognized a need in her life that I had been blind to for years. While still in that attitude of prayer, I asked God's forgiveness and help. The next day I began to make the appropriate change in behavior toward her. What a difference it has made! I am convinced that is how God may speak to us when we are silent before Him.

57

Confidence In Responding To God

Listening to God will lead to actions as well as words. Words are just the beginning. If we're reading 1 Corinthians 15, for example, we will exalt the Lord for the great victory of the resurrection and the hope that goes with it.

Listen to these words of Paul in this great resurrection chapter:

Brethren, I declare to you the gospel which I preached to you, which also you received

*and in which you stand, by which you are
saved, if you hold fast that word which I
preached to you—unless you believed in
vain. For I delivered to you first of all that
which I also received: that Christ died for
our sins according to the Scriptures, and
that He was buried and that He rose again
the third day according to the Scriptures
(1 Corinthians 15:1-4).*

And later, "Now Christ is risen from the
dead, and has become the firstfruits of those who
have fallen asleep. For since by man came death,
by Man also came the resurrection of the dead"
(vv. 20-21).

But our response will go beyond simply being
excited about the truth of the passage.

• It will give us greater confidence as we face
a defeated spiritual enemy.

• It will give us words to say to the termi-
nally ill.

• It will give us power as we face the

58

everyday tumults of life.

• It may cause us to forsake a sinful attitude or habit.

When we pray, we must be ready to take action. The deeper the prayer goes into the Scripture, into the mind of God, the more radical the action may be. It may lead us to someone's living room to share a deep burden. It may carry us back into the past to deal with some unresolved hurt we have received or inflicted. It may drastically change our plans. We may end up in some strange place doing things we never thought we would or could do. This is because our prayer is to God, and He is not a placid, inert Being. He is the living God who steps into our lives with His awesome power and changes us in dramatic and unpredictable ways as we respond to Him. Or He may leave us right where we are. That's okay. He's God!

When we bow before God with our needs and our requests, we think we're the initiators. But it may well be that all prayer is a response to Him. This is what Norway's Ole Hallesby taught in his classic book, *Prayer.* He saw Jesus' words "Behold, I stand at the door and knock" (Revelation 3:20) as the key that opens the door to prayer. And how does Christ knock? Through the conditions and circumstances of our experience that drive us to Him in prayer. As I think of it, my prayers for little Nathan were a response. Jesus had been knocking on the door of my life through the physical needs of my grandson.

60

D | Defer To God's Perspective

You've had something similar to this happen to you, I'm sure: You call the auto dealer and ask for the service department to check on your car in the shop. "Can you hold?" the cheerful voice asks. In a few seconds the "elevator music" starts. Every so often a recording assures you that your call is "very important to us" and that it will be answered in the order it was received. You imagine dozens of others on their phones, just hoping for a chance to talk to an actual human. You wait and wait, imagining that an inane conversation about last night's ball game or some television program is keeping you in limbo. After a while you're ready to hang up. It would take less time to get in your other car and drive over to the place!

Sometimes, doesn't it seem that God has put us on hold?

He may be doing some great things in our lives, but our deepest, most cherished request is not being granted. We know He's still there, but He is simply not responding. What is going on?

Hannah of the Old Testament knew what it was like to feel rejected by God (1 Samuel 1:1-18). She was one of two women married to a man named Elkanah. Peninnah, the other wife, had borne him children, but Hannah was barren in a day when childlessness was considered a sign of God's displeasure. To make matters worse,

Peninnah took cruel delight in mocking Hannah's barrenness whenever the family made their annual trip to the house of God to offer a sacrifice.

Even though Hannah was a devout and faithful woman, her distress lasted for years. She prayed and prayed. Yet God didn't answer. On one trip to the house of God "she was in bitterness of soul, and prayed to the Lord and wept in anguish" (v. 10).

But that is not the end of Hannah's story. In God's time, which was just the right time, God gave Hannah a son. She became the mother of Samuel (vv. 19-20), who in time would become a priest and prophet who would change the course of history.

In God's time, Hannah's sense of spiritual rejection was changed to joy and her bitterness was turned to trust. Later, in an overwhelming song of praise to God, Hannah showed that her deepest longing was not for a son but to know that she was accepted and approved by God.

My heart rejoices in the Lord; my horn is exalted in the Lord. I smile at my enemies, because I rejoice in Your salvation. No one is holy like the Lord, for there is none besides You, nor is there any rock like our God. Talk no more so very proudly; let no arrogance come from your mouth, for the Lord is the God of knowledge (1 Samuel 2:1-3).

For every generation to come, her experience would show that what counts is not whether God immediately answers our prayers. The issue is whether we are humbly waiting on His wisdom and timing—if we are willing to defer to God.

When Hannah's experience is combined with the rest of Scripture, we begin to see some of the many reasons for deferring not to our emotions but to the wisdom of God.

Confidence In God's Perspective

Our perspective is like looking through a pinhole. We can't see the whole picture. If we could, we would see that what we long for may not be good for us or for those we love. How many times I have been thankful that God has not given me everything I've asked Him for. How much better off I would have been if I had tempered my prayers with the awareness that it is only when we get to heaven that we will see the whole picture.

The apostle Paul tried to give us that perspective in the latter part of 1 Corinthians 13 when he said, "For now we see in a mirror, dimly, but then face to face. Now I know in part, but then I shall know just as I also am known" (vv. 12-13). While God knows us fully and completely now, we will not understand God and know His perspective completely until we are in heaven. For now, we must have confidence that in God's perspective of our circumstances and needs.

Scottish theologian P. T. Forsythe wrote, "We shall come one day to a heaven when we shall gratefully see that God's great refusals were sometimes the truest answers to our prayers."

Confidence In God's Wisdom

God knows our deepest need.

I heard a story about a single mother who was struggling to pay her bills and take care of her children. So she prayed for $2,000 to bring her financial relief. God denied the request as she expressed it. Instead of giving her the money, God gave her a job that she could handle. Then He gave her a friend who helped her to learn to manage her finances.

65

In time she was able to look back and see that God did answer her request, but in a way that reflected His wisdom. The best part is that she grew in her trust in God.

Confidence In God's Timing

The house sells later than we wanted or the baby arrives two weeks sooner than we expected. God's timing is always best because of His ability to orchestrate the circumstances of our lives.

Think again about Hannah and her longsuffering in prayer. In her mind, she must have surely thought that God was mistaken in not giving her a child during the years when she was being provoked by Peninnah (1 Samuel 1:7). However, God needed Samuel to be born at just the time he was born so he could be taught by Eli and later become God's prophet during the time he was needed in Israel's history.

Confidence In God's Goodness

We may have prayed a long time for our wife or husband to treat us with more respect, but perhaps that does not happen until God leads us to stop downgrading our spouse in public.

There are many reasons the answer has not come. Perhaps we are refusing to forgive someone, or we are controlled by an obsession, or we are seething in such anger that our holiness is corrupted. Or we "ask amiss" so that we can indulge some base desire (James 4:3). We need to do the work of examination, confession, and repentance before our prayer is answered.

Oswald Chambers understood that waiting is part of prayer. About the verse, "Men always ought to pray and not lose heart" (Luke 18:1), he wrote:

> Jesus taught His disciples the prayer of patience. If you are right with God and God delays the answer to your prayer, don't misjudge Him. Don't think of Him as an unkind friend, or an unnatural father, or an unjust judge, but keep at it. Your prayer will certainly be answered, for "everyone who asks receives." Pray and do not cave in. Your heavenly Father will explain it all one day. He cannot just yet because He is developing your character. "Forget the character," you say. "I want Him to grant my request." And He says, "What I am doing far exceeds what you can see or know. Trust Me."

The psalmist Asaph learned to overcome such disillusionment when he was reminded of the wider perspective of God. In Psalm 73 he said:

*Truly God is good to Israel, to such as are
pure in heart. But as for me, my feet had
almost stumbled; my steps had nearly slipped.
For I was envious of the boastful, when I
saw the prosperity of the wicked. For there
are no pangs in their death, but their strength
is firm. They are not in trouble as other
men . . . . Surely I have cleansed my heart
in vain, and washed my hands in innocence.
For all day long I have been plagued, and
chastened every morning. If I had said, "I
will speak thus," behold, I would have been
untrue to the generation of Your children.
When I thought how to understand this, it
was too painful for me— until I went into
the sanctuary of God; then I understood
their end. Surely You set them in slippery
places; You cast them down to destruction.
Oh, how they are brought to desolation, as
in a moment! They are utterly consumed
with terrors. As a dream when one awakes,*

68

*so, Lord, when You awake, You shall despise
their image. Thus my heart was grieved, and
I was vexed in my mind. I was so foolish
and ignorant; I was like a beast before You.
Nevertheless I am continually with You; You
hold me by my right hand. You will guide me
with Your counsel, and afterward receive me
to glory. Whom have I in heaven but You?
And there is none upon earth that I desire
besides You. My flesh and my heart fail;
but God is the strength of my heart and my
portion forever (Psalm 73:1-5,13-26).*

69

E | **Enjoy God While You Wait**

The psalmist Asaph showed us that there is
more to trusting God than deferring to His
wisdom. Notice in Psalms the descriptions of the
comfort Asaph enjoyed in God's presence:

- God holds me by my right hand
- God will guide me with His counsel.

- There is none . . . that I desire besides You.
- God is the strength of my heart.

These elements of comfort in God's presence can lead us to another way to become confident in prayer: We can learn to actually enjoy Him while waiting for Him to meet our needs. Think about it like this: Nothing we are waiting for can begin to compare with the profound privilege of knowing Him and being with Him. Nothing else is as important to us as God Himself.

Certainly there are times when we will be overwhelmed by our troubles and crushed by our sense of disappointment and grief. Like Hannah, we will have times when we are beside ourselves with frustrated longings because we don't know God's timetable. Yet there will also be many other times when we can laugh for joy—not just because of what God is doing for us—but because our prayer brings us close to Him in an enjoyable relationship.

And that confidence is enhanced as we

think about our knowledge of Him and His promises to us.

Confidence In What You Know About Him

As we learn to wait for God, we can begin to find delight in what we already know about Him. A complete accounting of all we know and love about God is too exhaustive for this study, but a quick study of just the book of Psalms reminds us about many of the attributes of God that can give us confidence:

- God is our refuge and our strength (Psalm 46:1).
- God is the judge (Psalm 75:7).
- The Lord is good, ready to forgive, and full of mercy (Psalm 84:11).
- God is full of compassion (Psalm 86:15).
- The Lord is upright; there is no unrighteousness in Him (Psalm 92:15).
- The Lord is our defense and the rock of our refuge (Psalm 94:22).

- Strength and beauty are His sanctuary (Psalm 96:6).
- The Lord is good, His mercy is everlasting, and His truth endures to all generations (Psalm 100:5).
- The Lord is gracious and full of compassion (Psalm 111:4).
- The Lord is great (Psalm 135:5).
- The Lord is good to all (Psalm 145:9).
- God's understanding is infinite (Psalm 147:5).

Because of the greatness of our awesome heavenly Father as seen through these and many other passages of Scripture, we should eagerly accept the invitation of the psalmist to enter His gates with thanksgiving and His courts with praise, and to bless His name (Psalm 100:4).

Thank Him. God has done so much for you. If your boss or parents had done one-tenth that much for you, you would express your gratitude in lavish terms. Do the same with God.

O Lord my God, I will give thanks to You

forever (Psalm 30:12).

Jesus gave thanks to the Father (Luke 10:21). Paul's prayers were filled with expressions of gratitude (Ephesians 5:20). We too should give joyful thanks to the Lord.

Praise Him. We praise God for who He is and we thank Him for what He has done. The Bible is brimming with expressions of praise to the Lord.

Praise, O servants of the Lord, praise the name of the Lord! Blessed be the name of the Lord from this time forth and forevermore! From the rising of the sun to its going down the Lord's name is to be praised (Psalm 113:1-3).

Other passages of praise to the Lord include Psalm 146:1-2, Hebrews 13:15, and Revelation 4:11. Lift your praise up to God in your prayer. Express your worship and adoration in praise. "He is your praise" (Deuteronomy 10:21).

As we go to God in prayer, our confidence is enhanced because of the nature, characteristics, and attributes of the God of the universe.

Confidence In What He Has Promised

Another way to enjoy God is to rejoice in the promises He gives us about prayer. Paul named three promises in this classic prayer passage:

> *Be anxious for nothing, but in everything by prayer and supplication, with thanksgiving, let your requests be made known to God; and the peace of God, which surpasses all understanding, will guard your hearts and minds through Christ Jesus (Philippians 4:6-7).*

The Promise Of God's Peace. The antidote to anxiety is prayer. The commitment of God is that when we roll our burdens onto His shoulders, He will give us peace. Many Christians will testify that in the dark night of fear when they took their burden to the Lord, He gave them peace and they could sleep (Psalm 4:8). Therefore, we can rejoice in knowing that when we take our concerns and burdens and cares to the Lord, He will give us a peace that goes

74

beyond our human ability to comprehend it.

The Promise Of God's Protection. Our minds and hearts will be protected when we pray. He who is our fortress guards us when the enemy attacks: "For You are my rock and my fortress; therefore, for Your name's sake, lead me and guide me" (Psalm 31:1-3). With that in mind, we can rejoice in the protection we know He gives us.

The Promise Of God's Presence. Paul expressed it this way: "The God of peace will be with you" (Philippians 4:9). In our storm, while going through the valley, or when we feel the most alone, prayer reminds us of God's presence. We can rejoice in His promise to be with us wherever we may be.

75

PRAYING
THROUGH
the BIBLE

THE SCRIPTURES were written by people who felt the same desires and faced the same discouragements we face. They too were dismayed at times by their circumstances. They knew what it was like to cry out to a seemingly silent God, to come to the end of themselves, and to feel their emotions going "over the edge." Yet the people of the Bible are important to us because they lived long enough to recover their sense of joy and confidence in God.

As we struggle through our own fears and

disappointments, we can find renewed hope by using their thoughts as a reflection of our own hearts and prayers. Psalm 42 is a good example. This psalm was written by someone who represented people who had been oppressed by an enemy. It appears that those affected were in exile and living among godless people who had no love of God and no concern for those who did love Him. The spiritual drought in such a land must have been terrible.

So with a thirsty, downcast soul, the author cried out to the Lord and expressed the honest emotions of his heart.

First we will quote a verse, and then we'll show how you might pray, based on what the verse says.

Psalm 42:1-2: "As the deer pants for the water brooks, so pants my soul for You, O God. My soul thirsts for God, for the living God. When shall I come and appear before God?"

Prayer: *Lord, those words express how empty I feel. I feel so dry and tired and weak from running. My strength is gone. I don't know how much longer I can go on. If You don't help me, I'm not going to make it.*

I know that someday I will stand before You. But I long to hear from You now. What do You want from me? What do You want me to do?

Psalm 42:3: "My tears have been my food day and night, while they continually say to me, 'Where is your God?' "

Prayer: *Father, I am often surrounded by those who don't know You, don't love You, don't even realize that You exist. This bothers me so much that sometimes I think about this instead of eating. I've been so open in the past about trusting You. But now I feel uncomfortable when I'm with people who don't share my love for You. Please restore my confidence in You.*

Psalm 42:4: "I used to go with the multitude; I went with them to the house of

God, with the voice of joy and praise."

Prayer: *Things used to be so different, Lord. I used to enjoy You in the presence of Your people. We laughed and prayed together. Yet now the circumstances have changed, and I feel so alone. Those times of joy seem so far away. Please restore to me the joy of fellowship with other believers.*

Psalm 42:5: "Why are you cast down, O my soul? And why are you disquieted within me? Hope in God, for I shall yet praise Him."

Prayer: *Yes, Father, I too know better. As I listen to my own complaint, I know deep inside that You can still be trusted. I do know that it is right to keep on trusting You. Like the psalmist, I even believe that in Your wisdom, and at the right time, You will help me. I know I will laugh again. I know the day is coming when I will praise You. O Lord, how I long for that day!*

Psalm 42:8: "The Lord will command His lovingkindness in the daytime, and in the

night His song shall be with me—a prayer to the God of my life."

Prayer: *I do believe that the day is coming when You will again let me experience Your kindness. I believe that You will once again give me songs in the night.*

Psalm 42:9: "I will say to God my Rock, 'Why have You forgotten me? Why do I go mourning?' "

Prayer: *Father, even though I know You will help me, my fears keep coming back over me like waves. In spite of my faith in You, and even though I know You are my rock and my hiding place, I still feel so forgotten and alone. Why do You have to let me, Your child, spend my time mourning rather than praising You?*

Psalm 42:11: "Why are you cast down, O my soul? And why are you disquieted within me? Hope in God; for I shall yet praise Him, the help of my countenance and my God."

Prayer: *I wonder, Lord, why I allow my*

circumstances to get me down—why my heart grows so heavy. Instead, I want to praise You, Lord, for You are my only hope. I praise You for Your goodness. Forgive me for doubting You. I will wait for You. I will wait for You to restore my joy!

With revitalized confidence, you can renew your joy and trust in God by praying through other passages of Scripture. The psalms, of course, are a rich resource for this kind of prayer. Other books that work well for this are the Proverbs and the New Testament letters, the Epistles.

For specific circumstances that occur in your life, the following list may be especially helpful.

Bible Passages To Pray Through When . . .

In Danger:
Psalm 91 ■ Key Verse: *"I will say of the Lord, 'He is my refuge and my fortress; My God, in Him I will trust"* (v. 2).

Depressed:

Psalm 34 ■ **Key Verse:** *"I sought the Lord, and He heard me, and delivered me from all my fears" (v. 4)*

Psalm 139 ■ **Key Verse:** *"Search me, O God, and know my heart; try me, and know my anxieties; and see if there is any wicked way in me, and lead me in the way everlasting" (vv. 23-24).*

Worried:

Philippians 4 ■ **Key Verse:** *"Be anxious for nothing, but in everything by prayer and supplication, with thanksgiving, let your requests be made known to God" (v. 6).*

Facing A Crisis:

Psalm 121 ■ **Key Verse:** *"My help comes from the Lord" (v. 2).*

Psalm 46 ■ **Key Verse:** *"Be still and know that I am God; I will be exalted among the nations" (v. 10).*

Discouraged:

Psalm 23 ▪ **Key Verse:** *"Yea, though I walk through the valley of the shadow of death, I will fear no evil; for You are with me" (v. 4).*

Psalm 42 ▪ **Key Verse:** *"Why are you cast down, O my soul?...Hope in God, for I shall yet praise Him" (v. 5).*

Isaiah 40 ▪ **Key Verse:** *"But those who wait on the Lord shall renew their strength" (v. 31).*

84

Tempted:

Psalm 1 ▪ **Key Verse:** *"Blessed is the man who walks not in the counsel of the ungodly . . . but his delight is in the law of the Lord" (v. 1).*

1 Corinthians 10:1-15 ▪ **Key Verse:** *"No temptation has overtaken you except such as is common to man; but God is faithful, who will not allow you to be tempted beyond what you are able, but with the temptation will also make the way of escape" (v. 13).*

Lonely:

Psalm 27 ■ **Key Verse:** *"When my father and my mother forsake me, then the Lord will take care of me" (v. 10).*

Needing Courage:

Joshua 1 ■ **Key Verse:** *"Have I not commanded you? Be strong and of good courage; do not be afraid, nor be dismayed, for the Lord your God is with you wherever you go" (v. 9).*

Seeking Forgiveness:

Psalm 32 ■ **Key Verse:** *"Blessed is he whose transgression is forgiven, whose sin is covered" (v. 1).*

Psalm 51 ■ **Key Verse:** *"Wash me thoroughly from my iniquity, and cleanse me from my sin" (v. 2).*

In Doubt:

Hebrews 11 ■ **Key Verse:** *"Now faith is the*

*substance of things hoped for, the evidence of
things not seen" (v. 1).*

Needing Assurance:

Romans 8 ■ **Key Verse:** *"Who shall separate
us from the love of Christ? Shall tribulation,
or distress, or persecution, or famine, or
nakedness, or peril, or sword?" (v. 35).*

1 John 5 ■ **Key Verse:** *"These things I have
written to you who believe in the name of the
Son of God, that you may know that you have
eternal life, and that you may continue to believe
in the name of the Son of God" (v. 13).*

Thankful:

Psalm 136 ■ **Key Verse:** *"Oh, give thanks
to the God of gods! For His mercy endures
forever" (v. 2).*

Psalm 103:1-13 ■ **Key Verse:** *"The Lord
is merciful and gracious, slow to anger, and
abounding in mercy" (v. 8).*

Joyful:
Psalm 100 ■ **Key Verse:** *"Make a joyful shout to the Lord, all you lands!" (v. 1).*

Looking for Direction:
John 14 ■ **Key Verse:** *"Jesus said..., 'I am the way, the truth, and the life. No one comes to the Father except through Me'" (v. 6).*

Your
NEXT
PRAYER

YOUR NEXT PRAYER could change your life. Go back to page 12. How did you fill in the blank? Are any of the disappointments on pages 14-16 affecting you?

It's time to act. Ask God to help you make the decision to push through those roadblocks, overcome those hindrances, and begin praying as you would like to. If you get discouraged, don't let that stop you. The Puritans had a saying, "Pray until you pray." Keep praying. You will soon pray with renewed confidence—and you'll find your trust in God and the joy of your salvation restored.

On the other hand, it could be that you need to start with the most basic step of all. Perhaps as you've read this booklet, you've sensed that you are not sure you have a personal relationship with God through Jesus Christ— that you have not experienced the salvation He offers to all who believe. You realize that you are a sinner (Romans 3:23), but you are not sure what to do about your sin—and about turning your life over to God.

Here are some important concepts you need to consider.

You cannot save yourself.

The Bible says, "For by grace you have been saved through faith, and that not of yourselves; it is the gift of God" (Ephesians 2:8-9). Paul was writing to a group of people who had trusted

Jesus Christ as Savior, and he was explaining that it was only because of God's grace in sending Jesus that they had been redeemed.

> **Jesus Christ, the sinless Son of God, lived the perfect life we could never live.**

The Bible says, "[Christ] committed no sin, nor was deceit found in His mouth" (1 Peter 2:22). Only a perfect person could present himself as the perfect sacrifice, acceptable to God as our substitute. And only Jesus was perfect.

> **Jesus died on the cross to pay the penalty for all our sin.**

The Bible says, "For I delivered to you first of all that which I also received: that Christ died for our sins according to the Scriptures, and that He was buried, and that He rose again the third day according to the Scriptures" (1 Corinthians 15:3-4). Jesus not only died for our sins—taking all of our sins on His shoulders—but He also rose from the dead to show His power over death.

Christ's resurrection is proof that His sacrifice was acceptable to God.

The Bible says, "Grace to you and peace from Him who is and who was and who is to come, . . . and from Jesus Christ, the faithful witness, the firstborn from the dead, and the ruler over the kings of the earth. To Him who loved us and washed us from our sins in His own blood" (Revelation 1:4-6).

We receive the Lord as our Savior by faith.

The Bible says, "For God so loved the world that He gave His only begotten Son, that whoever believes in Him should not perish but have everlasting life" (John 3:16).

Ask God to save you from the deserved

92

penalty of your own sins. Trust Him to rescue you. You will find that this request will be the most important prayer you will ever pray. It is this prayer for salvation that provides an unshakable foundation for all of the other prayers you will ever offer up to God.

If you do put your sincere faith in Jesus Christ, you become a child of God, an heir to His kingdom in heaven. At that point, you also have opened to you the avenue of prayer—of fellowship with God. Now when you pray, you will be communicating with the God of the universe—and He will hear you.